THE FOUR-DOORED HOUSE

The Four-Doored House

~

PIERRE NEPVEU

TRANSLATED FROM THE FRENCH BY
DONALD WINKLER

THE POETRY IMPRINT AT VÉHICULE PRESS

Published with the generous assistance of the Canada Council for the
Arts, the Canada Book Fund of the Department of Canadian
Heritage, and the Société de développement des entreprises
culturelles du Québec (SODEC).

Canada Council   Conseil des arts
for the Arts   du Canada

Signal Editions editor: Carmine Starnino
Cover design: David Drummond
Typeset in Minion and Filosofia by Simon Garamond
Photo of author: Karine Prévost-Nepveu
Printed by Livres Rapido Books

Originally published as *L'espace caressé par ta voix*
©Éditions du Noroît 2019

LIBRARY AND ARCHIVES CANADA CATALOGUING IN PUBLICATION
Title: The four-doored house / Pierre Nepveu ; translated from the
French by Donald Winkler.
Other titles: Espace caressé par ta voix. English
Names: Nepveu, Pierre, author. | Winkler, Donald, translator.
Description: Translation of: L'espace caressé par ta voix. | Poems.
Identifiers: Canadiana (print) 20220481288 | Canadiana (ebook)
20220481318 | ISBN 9781550656237
(softcover) | ISBN 9781550656305 (EPUB)
Classification: LCC PS8577.E55 E8713 2023 | DDC C841/.54—dc23

Published by Véhicule Press, Montréal, Québec, Canada

Distribution in Canada by LitDistCo
www.litdistco.ca
Distribution in US by Independent Publishers Group
www.ipgbook.com

Printed in Canada on FSC certified paper.

On the margins of the page
the crimson light flares up
with all things still to come
with all things born to die.

RACHEL KORN

Memories debark from the future
to embrace my shadow.

FRANÇOIS CHARRON

Contents

I

Futures

For Lily, born in 2016

Return from the Plains

Towards evening the Saskatchewan sky rolled over us, pouring down heat and haze to mark our return from a long expedition alongside salt ponds. The fields of colza had dusted you with pollen, you'd trekked the forest, calling out along the way to elk avid for bark and sap. You had not yet sorted out your words, you charmed cats with your flurried voice and your fragrance drove dogs giddy. Dictates of right reason, sound judgment, swept through you like a cloud. You told no tales, could barely sing, mostly laughed and wept, hummed like an eighteen-wheeler, and took by storm my orphan piano, mindless of trills and arpeggios, bent on hammering whites and blacks, your will to brightness prevailing over all. The world kept its distance from you, so beset it was by dark forces and rumblings remote-controlled by furor or disquiet, this world where you existed so stoutly yet counted for so little, you too absolute, too luminous for its shadow play, sovereign in your joy, imperious in your beauty.

You do not recognize yourself in the photos taken at rest stops by your mother. You didn't see the mountains of gravel coursing down in a dry season's deadpan air, the herds of trucks rolling up to the Qu'Appelle River and its heavenly harvests, their drivers plagued by homesickness and a thirst for women. A video shows you roaming a supermarket's gorges, pondering its cliffs, a plastic crow perched high on cereal boxes while a nasal voice reels off the day's specials. Later, by the roadside, picnic tables are backed up against the forest, the trees marking time, a distilled century below their bark, years of carbon and burnished rails, then you totter to a ditch where fireweed grows. Lilac time was short-lived, dense as a global enigma, transient in recall and prone to memory's lapses. Your childhood cannot resist the forces of evil and beauty's high winds. But you are wholly present and all vowels find a nest within you, crucible of legends, omnipotent abyss.

You stayed in a Grande Prairie hotel room
for a night as empty of dreams
as the prairie is poor in trees.
For days you'd roamed your fathers' land
with your mouth tasting of juneberries or saskatoons,
and returning you'd see in Wawa
the phantom storm god
batter North Ontario rocks.
You worked your legs and tried out languages,
said *daddy* and *maman*,
poised precariously between you and you,
and heedless of those around you
walked blithely down the hotel hallway
to pace out time and space,
joy in motion.

You will say, this is how I imagine the journey I've wholly forgotten. I entered the mirror to emerge multiple. In the prairie I found hidden stones, ancestors' voices, the first intimations of cold at summer's end. A poet revealed to me animals under the earth. I heard a commotion, I thought, of barks and cries. In one fell swoop the land revived ancient pain, warriors bleeding amid the grain, women giving birth, children who, crying, combed the underbrush when autumn was already transforming the forest into a crystalline orchestra where sounded the arctic season's icy brass. The wind acquired a wintery voice that tried my courage. Father and mother, you did not know that I was too tiny for so much past.

Is it the deepness of the earth that drew you? Those eons of shards and bones? Or the pristine surface of a first snow, nearest to the sky where late birds stir, clouds of asterisks loosed by angels? You don't even remember acceding to your zone of all blessings, where the cyclopean train roars and trees like old bones splinter.

I dreamed, you told me, of a door opening onto snow, in a month whose name I did not know. To what species is it kin, that which runs on, leaving signs in its wake? To that of things that move, that are shapes in motion, shaggy and warm to the fingertips. Dogs that rest and sleep. Their faces, their ears, their teeth. A genus with eyes that open to beg forgiveness and ask for tenderness. Seekers of love. On my knees, I am she who gives. In the night I hear them snore, huff, groan. The night is a great dog dream that has forgotten my hands, chasing after shadows and reclaiming the desire to bite, the right to wound.

You foresaw the September snows
that often fall there, those chills
rife with prairie dogs and their white breath,
their puppet heads. You learned
that even frost has its populace
and is strewn with signs that lend it speech,
its breath that holds to stones
and to soaring enduring woods,
and at times a rodent's anxious existence
reminds us that the world's a wheel
on which we dance
and that we always return
to the fold. Yours was still a cloud,
a composition with no name
blessed by the sun and overrun
with the coppered dust of afternoons
where your mother's warm breast
was your only address, cheek by jowl with paradise.

And it was sometimes a return to whiteness
softened by rain, laid down in fog,
a sweetness come drifting, elusive
in February, season of a hundred faces,
and you were there to stammer your alphabet
and dance to Brazilian airs
all through your second winter,
muttering skewed words, piling up
blocks of square letters
before dusk when stories awoke
and breathed black forest magic through the house.
You didn't yet know that tales are made from letters
and syllables and that even fright may be written down.
You mouthed the élan vital of voices to come
that would articulate within you desires and regrets,
combats and treasons, but that would express
the colour of your world—and that too
might be written down.

The lofty stuff of the soul,
the aspiration to be more than oneself
that I detected in your eyes
that saw the world as alien
and perceived it as separate parts
like a perplexing mechanism,
your one finger to turn off or on,
your obsession with open boxes,
your passion for departures and farewells,
your obliviousness to deep water
when beneath the rippling reflections
you could not foresee the risks,
and how to instruct you in the feelings of grass
faced with the laws of frost
and the apathy of the willows
before November's ferocity?
All this world in me, like a gaping hole,
a language to relearn.

Here is where you begin, still ignorant of the name you share with that small flower. Your life is a breath of apple, of light welling up from a finger, of the father's sleep from which you emerge with tousled hair, dazzled by the firebird flying across the room. There is a secret in the sheets, a mystery in the carpet, and in the yard a dead tree that no longer answers calls. You don't know what binds the squirrel to flight, and you are gripped by fear when faces change and passions are on the boil. On rue Maisonneuve, the train from the west sets you to trembling.

Because of you I came to love the word *channel*,
where birds and the wind at times do thread their way.
I thought of you who would chart yourself a destiny
among rocks, wrecks, islets
of structures archaic after thirty years.
Since our adieus to the industrial age
we've had to skim the water's surface. I saw you already
tapping out messages on your cell phone,
your whole life on a tactile screen
to which you would consign both love and hate,
navigating the universe's narrow gorges,
plucking sparks of truth out of the scorching air.

The Four-doored House

The four-doored house
was so small that yourself
you could not fit into it.
You slipped in a groping hand,
it filled all of an empty room.
We might have thought there was something
you were trying to ensnare,
an insect, a mote of dust,
a simple breath of air.
You wanted to reel all in,
even the invisible.

In the four-doored house
no memories have yet been inscribed,
there are no ancient wardrobes
nor chests with old records,
no regrets slamming their heads
against cold walls.
The house has no real windows,
no dust bunnies
adrift under the furniture, no chair
in which to dream, no bed lamps
for books of love and war.
She's just waiting for what is to come,
the world seems far away
but in truth it is very near,
that fire outside that wants to enter in.

The future of the four-doored house
is shaped by the prose of daily life.
Dividers there segregate study from pleasure,
light veers compliant to seasons and days
over open books that will swallow the night
while the heartache of living can seal itself off
in a shut room where music's ablaze.
In the kitchen, the ghost of a lavish hand
that drew graters and knives from the drawers.

I seek you through the four-doored house:
is it just me who feels at home?
I found there a narrow table on which to work,
to reread *Sources of the Self* and *La mesure de l'homme*
and to rework sight unseen my map of hope,
but you don't arrive, you're outside
despite the cold and scraps of news on the prowl,
with your dog you cross the road and
I wonder when you might come in to sit
and if the light that allows me to read
will one day beam
from your bright eyes alone.

Entering the four-doored house
you found the sun all in shards
of shattered glass. An interior is at times
just fingers bleeding into a basin
and drawers slammed shut on objects of worship.
It's from here that the outside seems free of flaws
and locked-down lands, as if birds
never harmed themselves
on hedges or ledges
and to breathe in strong wind forestalled
thought's stoppages and the heart's contractions.

A puddle of milk on the floor
of the house. Is it your exuberance,
your clumsiness, or rather your yen
for a tenanted disorder where flies buzz,
where steaming meals tease the evening air?
A nomadic family came by, you were
the friend of the little girl, she remembered
being cold on the icy path
but entering your kitchen
she drank warm milk and it made her smile.

Rumour has it that elsewhere in the city there are
other empty houses with no street and no address.
Gaunt men come to sleep there,
grey fatigue beneath their skin,
yet they are happy to see dawn light creep in at the window,
those who have room
only for the cold and for whom neither the sun
nor men as visitants draw near.

Perhaps you will know it one day:
there was a time when just the advent of an angel
set water in vases to trembling,
walls silently opened to the beyond
as in a Tintoretto canvas
with breached surfaces, forced entry of the divine
for a beautiful young woman with bowed head,
knowing herself visited by a presence,
small house, woman's body, windswept words
declaring a turning point for the world.

You summon love to a four-doored house:
there where a childhood teeming with corn flakes,
ice cubes plopped into lemonade,
chocolate animals melted on the tongue,
are all meted out in spoonfuls of affection.
After a year of choreographing small objects,
you've discovered the rarity of a caressed cheek.

Near to the animals that sleep through the afternoon,
the jewels that come alive when you wear them,
the beads that roll and drop from the table
when you're tired of counting them, near
to the songstress on CD who threads her life
through a song and her voice that knives into you
in the four-doored house.

For some time there have been rocks
fattening in the cellar,
raccoons vexing the night
in the garden where are buried
your dog's ashes,
and when down there you see
the years you must scale, you think:
I was a simple little girl
who held in her hands
the four-doored house.

And abruptly your body has fled its noises,
left its odours and blocks
on the floor, for you speak all at once
of this light through the window
intruding on sentences you can barely
complete. For you don't know
where your ideas are heading,
and your clarity deserts you to glow
on the table where the quartered oranges lie
that you bite into while listening to noises
come from away, from a world more than ever
alien, while you are edging into your truth,
this urge to speak, the better to take in
the four-doored house's walls.

The house is emptied of everything,
me, my whims, my books.
I sleep in the back yard all day long,
rolled into a ball at the corner of the fence.
I hear the squirrels passing by
two steps away from my closed eyes.
I wake to ants,
hear far off your hairdryer mooing,
I wonder where you're going tonight
or if you're not more philosopher than me,
who thinks there's wider space within
than without.

Yet it's so simple, the sheet opened out
so as to swim through the dream-filled night,
the night table where you keep
an old magazine that talks of stars,
the dresser where the folded laundry lies,
the wool touched and stroked like a cat,
and the lavender-scented cotton
that has you trembling just to be alive on a winter's night.

A door opens where there is music,
then I see you exit your room,
a truant with ruby nails deserting
your toys paled from use,
your dolls bereft of eyes
there by your house's fourth door,
while behind you your father and mother,
leaning on the wind,
see you consort with the violence in the world.

I see through the window the dust of my years
clouding the future: two thousand and thirty-four,
you're eighteen years old, but how to conceive
of this time of abrasives and charred grasses
without your coolness casting its shadow over my bed,
without my wasting away being watched over by your eyes.
Am I still there to hear you?
My future absence is full with your voice,
I wonder what languages you speak,
and if one of them has you dreaming when you tell
of your grandfather and the four-doored house.

Human life remains homeless,
and when I come to you through the meandering
of my thoughts over rocky ground and sand,
I find you with neither house nor home nor the least repose,
doors and windows slam where time rushes in
smacking of landscapes riddled
with the sorrows of the poor and the pride of the mighty.
I see love hollowing out within you mad distances
and misjudging more raised walls far off:
empty gazes, chainmail, armed intentions,
I see rockfalls of flesh and feeling
in your room where you take refuge,
a brittle house overcome by voices
calling on one to leave, return, always
to return and never to put an end to the returning.

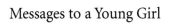

Messages to a Young Girl

If our thoughts sometimes lose their thread
and our sentences fill
with currents of air, is this a failure of the soul
or a dearth of dignity in chaos's face?
I cannot answer in your place,
nor claim that affinities and complicities
suffice, however frank and forthright.
Still, I've come down under the trees
to await you where on a day of rest I'd promised you
this humid transit on a May afternoon
in the Morgan forest where the flower fairy
breathes clouds into the plum trees.
I saw you, a little girl in rainboots
on the edge of a ditch, facing a clearing
where there would be no harvest, a butterfly
seeking to lodge in your hair.
You were the most guilelessly in the world
an open question under the grey sky,
you inhaled the earth's dampness
as if language and its anxieties
were but a needless luxury.

Often I think of the steps you sow
that I cannot see, more and more I weigh in my hand
your body's verve and the substance of my voice.
Has your youth outpaced me for good and all
when you venture into the city by the light
of LEDs that probe each night
the dusk? Not knowing, I speak
to my many-fingered shadow,
a ghost with hair on end
from news of drownings or of carnage,
slave to the doubts I feel encroaching,
a pall of malfeasance,
and the myths of cathodic screens
where happiness is hyped.
Now it's night and at the window
I see the garden trussed
to its sleeping wood, held hostage
by the long-knived moon,
might I still talk to you in darkness
and hope that the blade of time
will not lance my skin?

What you wanted to lob from the window
is not yourself or your sun-drunk dog
and its animal illusion
of unalloyed presence.
It is, in a mad lust for release,
all that fossilizes in your boxes:
your small pebbles gleaned on the beach,
your gimcrack jewels, your secret papers,
your dresses and blouses with angels' wings,
their colours rebuking
your glooms and even those marks
etched into your skin,
your life story to leaf through
like a novel in your post-midnight fevers.
"This age demands purity," you no doubt thought
as did I—and I knew, one day of tumult,
at your first love's emergency exit,
that you were at last going to strip yourself down,
shed your music, your scarves,
your messaged t-shirts, your nail polish.
You would have fewer sounds, fewer words
to express yourself, and later I would find you seated,
wrapped in a simple blanket
at the Place des Festivals one summer evening,
become almost a nun, levelling
your existence, limiting your possessions.
I would pass by you just like that
in hopes that merely by laying bare your courage
you are sending me a sign: things will be all right…

The great griefs that have befallen
I would have liked to spare you their narrative,
as if one could shift the wind's direction
or run the clocks backwards.
We were in New York on its tallest tower,
in Kigali before the rush of blood,
in Port-au-Prince on the eve of the crumbling,
at the Aleppo market to buy lemons and figs,
thinking to breathe in peace as one inhales fresh air,
crossing through forests before the fire,
fields of wheat with their intrusions of sand,
suburbs sealed off from the deluge,
I would have been your guide. But all was false,
humanity was reapplying its makeup,
music played on in the cellars
and tunnels that amplified the voice.
There was no before or after,
but disaster's legacy dogged me,
impossible to transmit, impossible to efface.

I found you matured and calmer on certain days,
a gardener of space, almost happy
despite the alarm bells' clamour
and the torrid heat of tainted debates.
Your own future now enlists me as a witness,
who thought to save myself listening to Schubert,
trailing my baggage along the philosophers' lane
from Kyoto to Toronto, autumns of the great enlightenment
when each landscape was a shelter for the mind.
You smile at me now with indulgence,
not disclosing the keys to your own wisdom,
nor the secret of the seedlings that will shower our rooftops
with the blessings of thyme and coriander
where the four winds meet, almost having us
forget our narrowness and our ice-bound reasoning.

Life expectancy is a notion half way between
the law of large numbers and religious faith.
I don't know if I'm talking to you to surrender to time
or to stay its course. I roam rue Sainte-Catherine
as on the nights of my adolescence.
I follow you into stores and bars
and trail you into the shadow consuming subway
to surface into Vendôme Station's glacial air—
where are you? Me, a soul in pain, nowhere's idler,
with hospital thoughts, green thoughts
like the rooms where fate flickered,
where hope had its own machines,
would I not have been the smooth talker
of your apprentice years,
a squatter in your late twenty-first century?
And yet I find you again pacing
rue Maisonneuve over the virgin snow
where your rumpled silhouette glides.
I'll be able to tag along a little and talk to you
like one who went before
groping his way on the road of unanswered questions.

There were tall glass columns,
banks and boutiques had reopened, the snow
had drawn in its claws and its black teeth
and before the stores stylish young women
did dance steps seeing their glorious beauty
in the revolving doors.
You were perhaps among them, but now
I only recognized your voice,
the way words pulsed in your throat
though your way of saying them had not changed,
while the world advanced its barriers
of gleaming metal and shatterproof glass
in its haste to keep money flowing
and to exhaust its reserves before nightfall.
I went near, I heard all languages
and I hoped to hear yours, which I'd seen
merge grammars and lexicons,
blending wide prairie and fluvial grace.
I remembered your infant's babbling
and the day you made this confession:
"When you will be old, very very old,
and torn jeans will no longer be in fashion,
when polymer will cover streets and roads
and the city will be a crystal bouquet
where meditation will pay a high price
for the object of its pieties and its nests of light,
I will speak to you in my softest voice, I will be alert
to your lapses of memory and I will take your arm
so that you will not go alone into the night."

You will not believe me if I tell you
that my mornings are at times so bereft
that the sky is an old soiled cloth
and my dictionaries themselves
are strongboxes for which I've lost
the combination. You would not comprehend
this torpor of an insect-gnawed tongue,
speech for you is a future in song,
the world burgeons beneath your fingers,
your syllables pulse,
you are embarking on a first philosophy
of presence and absence, of here
and there, and you know the sounds
that describe what drifts away and denotes
departure. So let us go together
to walk in the snow beneath the trees,
to see the water still atremble upon the river
and the elves in the mist
while the sumacs have shed
their blood and the willows
are frozen fountains where the moon comes to drink.
Know that for you too words will one day fail,
you will be mute before your misfortunes
when life's vise grips you close,
when love does not bear its fruits,
and the world's colours have paled.
You will face the wall of silence
and will remember my helplessness face to face with words
and how I envied your burgeoning speech,

and so you will rename beings and things,
you will speak of our promenades
and our silences beside the frozen stream.

Did you hear the sobbing beneath the earth,
the prayers of bodies laid down in their absence?
With you I followed the winding path
that with all its detours wards off death.
We had come to the end
of cadastral lands and commercial crossroads,
had seen peter out the beige grey streets,
the suburbs of coyotes with ember eyes
watched over by dogs and surveillance systems,
and now we were at the foot of Saint-Hilaire
where memory's sacrament hovered above
at the door to a church where the spirit dwelt,
with the steep slope seeking the sky far off.
Once your mother came there
with a Chinese lady afraid of falling,
and from high on Sugar Loaf the plain
seemed so vast beneath our eyes,
like a great book overwhelmed
by the story you would read one day
or perhaps never, too lost
in the haze of signs and urgent missives,
flattened hard against the panes of the day to day
with no ear any more to lend
to the prayerful weeping under the earth.

My sole mythology was that of the evangelists.
I remember God the Father,
the Son, the Holy Ghost, then let me
speak to you of ancient tales
and the adoring emanations that clouded
nuns' souls and woke the prayerful.
I will lead you on a pilgrimage to this bygone
world. I picture you in another life,
you would have lived in Compostella or perhaps in Tours
at a time when children in the countryside
talked to wolves on the edges of forests.
I see you inhaling great stirrings of the soul,
you are praying in yesteryear's snows, exulting
in the divinity of sunflowers and the torment of vines,
espousing religion without having been a mother,
coveted by the night where the burning bush is aflame.
You know nothing of the trials to come,
the mauve scars and bruised loins,
the stigmata that daub the skin
and signal piety deep in a raw-boned winter,
and one morning you will pack your bag
to embrace your being's sublime diminishment,
become a snow-white insomniac
stretched out on hard wood, dreaming
the four seasons' lover will come
to wake you from your pain.

Was it Montreal or was it Bulgaria
as an artist friend imagined it,
this alleyway swaddled in leafage
held tight to its pale wooden fences,
its birdhouses and its sheds
filled with harrows and rakes,
summer in this hallowed neighbourhood
where Notre-Dame bestowed its blessings,
its miracle of ice that fell from heaven.
But all was to change, your mother was nine years old,
it was before computer scares, falling
towers and the extinction of species.
The trees are old men in your part of town,
their twisted limbs scare little girls,
but the alleys are still like village lanes
somewhere on the Black Sea coast.
We'll journey if you like to Pomorie, to Primorsko,
we'll live in a little cabin
with a view of blue spindrift-flecked waves,
and we'll go out before nightfall onto the Côte Saint-Antoine,
amazed, dizzied from having travelled so far
without losing our faces or fears.

When you place your soft hands on the table
a May afternoon in a breath of sunshine
that is inclined to beguile men's moods,
do not forget that the one before you speaking
and declaring his love has known his own disquiet,
that he has walked paths that are poor and scrubby
and that he often still doubts his own mettle,
does not think his body is strength incarnate
when his knees give way and all his lacunae
beg for mercy, so when you hear his voice break during a confession,
issuing from a silence wider
than the empire of grammars and tales,
and when his words always liable to fall short
are the daughters of a tenderness he has not known,
consider that this flaw too makes him a man.

There are great clearings where you may study the magnolias
at the turning of cranky springtimes and decades
rife with knife attacks and vanished children.
Without me will you find your peace of mind
spread wide like a corolla, this roseate translucence
when leafage stays its birth?
What will you do with those passions that signal
the coming summer, constrained already by its evil demons,
its promises of peace lodged in the throat,
unless together we watch
magnolias opening up in the bare trees
and you ask me why such haste
and if the leaves have forgotten to be born.

You will one day know a feeling near to tears,
letting your dress drop to the floor
in a room where you're facing a man whose eyes are grey
or more and more green in the light of the lamp,
you would like body and soul to inhabit this day
and its nests of warmth enfolded between sheets
after the joyous tinkling of your jewels
where they fall like marbles onto the bedside table.
You will ask yourself if the work is done,
if time in this epoch has stopped
ringed round by its glass constructions,
if the roadways razed below you
are graveyards now or gardens.
You'll have veiled the dreary days
to enter love's domain,
which is not a single poem but phrases told like beads
numbering the temperateness of rooms,
bare hangers swaying in closets
where for an instant a scent of camphor fills your lungs,
before your feet reach out to probe the bedclothes' knoll.
Will you unstintingly embrace all that,
or will your ears go on paying heed
to history's heralds on the street,
pursuing the fly-by-night or a keening ambulance
whose occupant may be me
being conveyed on my urgent way
to an abiding silence?

Dust and Ash

Long before the fireworks
ushering in the twenty-second century, my body
will have lost its mass and its shape
and the cards displaying my photo,
my passport expiring in five or ten years,
will sleep yellowed in boxes
or deep in archives, and then the road
will be open for your wonderment
and if you find in my quarters rows
of clothes no longer worn,
odds and ends, old beach chairs,
rusted fans, skates and skis
long out of use,
and drawers filled with notes and scribbles,
you could clean house
and secure the bracing air you need to live,
for you there will be fevered summers and others
whose fumes will lacerate the rain,
sunny days for weddings,
November days for separations,
you'll come to know the school of ruptures and rebirths,
you will be broken and remade,
this future will embrace your being while I
will have lost my civil status and my words
will drop down orphaned, leaving my empty hands
and a mind that is nowhere or perhaps in you
like a murmur barely heard.

I came up with this plan, mad and strange:
to leave a trail not behind
but before us, as if my tale
led the way into the unknown, not seeking
survival or a share of your future
for a mock assurance of immortality,
but a promise that you on your own, young and alive,
might measure the world's fragility,
its landscape abraded by misery, the dead weight
of propagandas, and I would find you
less helpless the night
your resolve's tectonic plates will have shifted,
while your ear, deafened and alone,
senses a whispering by your side.

At times you yourself were the blank page
on which I laid out the course of my life,
you were my tale of small exaltations
preceding a decline. We walked through the woods
to comb the dense deeps of light,
your smile accented the nearness of my leaving
and your young girl's resolve to fathom
the strength in things, the imperatives of paths
that usher us through mists
and lay bare the bark's senescence.
I walked by your side in the penultimate
twilight that had us tilt
the way of shadows while endowing our words
with the tawny shades of epilogues.

Perhaps you no longer hear me,
all I say is now cocooned within,
my sentences reach no goal,
my only task is to sit in the garden
and decode my thoughts' commotion.
But if you come you may unearth my words one by one,
they've the colour and resistance of tubers
and you may do with them what you will,
I don't know if it's still a language
or my life itself running off at the mouth,
putting down roots in the impenetrable muck.

The fustian of the word *future*
leaves you cold, we've seen
the roads' gravel fly off as dust
and sought our journey's meaning on Google in vain,
so if you like, let us return
to what holds its peace and let us call on the infinitesimal,
small words know no typos,
you can rattle them in your hands like dice,
they fall beyond the table, beyond the city,
they roll on fallow slopes,
you held them in your hand when you were tiny
unaware that fate itself
wants all things set down in capitals.

I have survived my persona, the one
you saw at celebrations,
your summer birthdays beneath the willows
seasoned with strawberries and melon
in front of the Father of All Mercies' church,
Saint-Augustin des Irlandais,
with our red balloons tugging towards the sky.
I've seen the error of my worldly ways,
repented the abuses and humiliations
that gnawed at my joints and scored my skin,
you showed me many more months of August
with sizzling meat and fish,
and as the revelry grew
the more clandestine was my face, the one
absent from assemblies
but that kept watch behind my eyes,
the secret agent of a thousand photos
waiting in ambush behind smiles,
there where no one would know me,
not even you who seemed at times
to sense my presence in the way of animals
who sniff out the merest sadness
in their masters' scent.

The days' snowflakes grace your head:
a free fall of time gone by,
buildings barely risen,
their brittle bones assailed
by battering rams, capital gains,
while gas belches through
groundwater, so please
wash this squall from your brow,
splash warm water onto reddened cheeks,
forget the tales and tortured paths
with their springtimes scarred by one last freeze
and the revival of cruelties we thought lapsed.
Cleanse yourself and let my epoch decamp,
it knew the allure of sleekness
and aerodynamic curves,
but don't think you can infer more from that
than schoolings in bad faith,
a devious way of walking, an array
of splendid confessions to secure one's honour
when the next day's pills were exhausted
and we were overrun by picture books
paying homage to the plants and animals
that were our final solution
to the problem of evil and errant intentions.

The future is a garden of metaphors,
you alone walk there with an authentic visage
and a body bent on inhaling the earth.
Far off, on the age's frontiers,
forests and the wind are but likenesses
on a horizon of glaciers melting
to fulfil the prophecies,
you are the truest tale in this phantom garden
and if the carnations tremble when I imagine
reaching them out to you on the cusp of your eighteenth year,
it is due only to my fear that already,
become dust and ash,
I may lack the body and hands
to gather and offer you flowers.

My limbs are now spent,
my breath dispersed to the four horizons,
you don't know how they may recast my moods,
the loves of a man my age,
you can't conceive of the fates of bodies
as they access their better tomorrows
and a pale warmth strokes their backs
whispering this is the last
before the chill sets in, but know all the same
that I'm not blind to your suffering or your rage,
that I divine beneath your zest for life
wide landscapes of joy poorly defined,
passions for the absolute that have neither the words
nor the strength to displace furniture by night
or to wring out insomnia's damp cloths.
For now I am alone in time,
a man on the heights who is eating himself away,
and offers you little wisdom or reason, just
the conviction that time now and again veers towards madness,
towards the fever of afternoon sheets and the unbearable
sweetness of a body adored.

May he or she who has never penned
a bad poem forgive me,
may those who have never harboured
a vulgar thought cast the first
slur and return to the world of words,
I confess to being elsewhere on this chill morning
of an April ever true to its own cruelty,
grass-stingy and leading its horses
through low snow, their pale breath
like a suburban fog.
Is this the whim of a mind on the run,
or my reason scouring the fields?
In the forthright clarity of these slipshod words,
I brush past pole fences seeking
a stream that burnishes its pebbles in the service of hope,
and if the wind is complicit with the textured
feelings of a finer intelligence,
history's substance is but vapour
and each of my steps is a labour
where I recast my strength and my future.
My voice is foreign in this forest
which is never far distant at the end of my table
and this path that half-opens at the sound of my voice,
all at once more real than my gravest concerns
since within to without time is so short
that the poem has made the most of its chance
to exist, this flare of light where the trees write
their farewell letter, where the cold wind
brings me back to the land of men

there, just over my shoulder,
while far off in the snowy field
the last horse calls to me still.

I search for my tools in vain. I go down
into the cellar of the four-doored house,
there's a stench of fuel oil and life cast off,
a red-hot pipe spasmatic.
I find neither hammer nor dowels,
but I feel next to my chest a pen
that has leaked and stained my shirt.
I wave it in air that wants nothing of me.
I've lost a hundred poems in my pocket,
I hear them stirring and protesting:
word spills, blotches, noises
that no one will ever hear. I find
the strength to climb back up and see
if you're there, if the furniture has been repaired
all on its own and if the doors still open.

I fling tiny words across the table
and I open them like oysters to see
if the word *sky* contains a pearl,
if summer bears in its folds enough bees
to quell rumours of famine.
I ask myself if to say *here* is sufficient
for the landscape to shimmer with tenderness,
but when with a sharp thwack I crack open the word *heart*,
I can only hear this silence of the deeps
that in the end commands me to remain.
I have come for the grand soirees' great banquet
before the night can gnaw me to the bone.

If you find dust in your clothes
it will perhaps be the ashes of my days,
a parcel of my body gone back to space.
If it leaves traces on your sleeve
or in the pocket of your coat
and a tragedy occurs, the earth
goes dry or the wind no longer thrills,
or the sea lifts high up from its plateaus,
come to see in the room where you sleep
if the cars are derailed on the way West
or a red giant is looming at dawn.
If foreigners are thrust back into tropical zones
for fear they will trample the crops,
or if deformed vegetables have sown fear,
shake your sleeve, dust off your arm,
don't think it's me—

                        and if later
you turn and look far back,
you will perhaps see me seated at my table,
my body's silhouette clinging to the morning
with a tad of the century's smoke in my throat,
barely able to reassemble piece by piece
the little apparatus of words and things,
each day bent on writing you my last letter,
my legacy of what's possible, my hymn to a future
already past, shifting books and pencils about,
switching on the lamp to warm my palm,
(light, late in life, becomes so human).
Know that it's in speaking low that I lit it so

without your discerning my face,
there is only this cloud where I carved out my years
and which became my truest endeavour.

II

Intervals

For C., in the present

I made holes in the landscape, told with pebbles,
strewn with vowels, tilled with books. I spilled out
bedroom drawers in a mad outlay of living,
but where was I and to what end? I tossed
my worn clothes into a tub, my husks
of warmth and needful care, but where was I
and in fact who? There was time lost,
mental blunders in reckoning updates
and I thought I heard behind me a blaze
consuming old pages, as if
the years themselves could go up in smoke,
and the stuff of being was flammable. I felt
there were yawning holes in the day's cartography
where I mislaid my shadows and close to deaf already
loosed a cry into your silken body,
where were you? And you came from where and when?
I who cared only for flesh
and the glow of flesh and the grace
of your breasts and what rose from your soul
and peppered and machine gunned my small occupied world,
I was going to be vast in your company given what was uttered
between the stones, the blades of grass, the limbs,
recumbent upon you as in an empty room
where my entire life
was scored into strips of skin.

I made holes in the landscape, off-loaded
was my critical mass, spaced out were the low notes,
I was all at once playing body and voice in a major key,
a cantata of intervals and quivering silences,
sprawling chords, floating ribs
where my wheezing respiration was that of an animal trapped
in a nasty fence or hitched up for work and labouring.
Still I was prepared for horses and fire,
freed from received wisdom and manuals
for assembling the scattered instances of life,
and it was suddenly you (who were you? come from what oblivion?)
intoning under the shower your formulas for forgiveness,
throwing wide your bed to great hymns of hope
as if Cohen's religious grace one winter day
echoed still between our lobes and my slackness
lost itself in your high voltage proximity,
the left side of my brain sworn to silence, the other
to sifting through the strands of happiness upon your face.

I made holes in the landscape, I'm the one
you heard digging and spading just at
the boundary of what's known. I spawn breaths of air,
I create rifts and I'm also the one
who late in the night perturbs your pawn shop locale,
your landslips of dresses and star-flecked shoes,
your tall doll house scaffoldings.
I gravelled my escape routes,
tossed sand into my cabinet of spells,
I who shot up each morning with my pens
fled the heart-sore computer screen
where young women honed home pages.
But you are there in your scarves, with your feasts,
we assemble in your rooms
with fragrant herbs and little candied words,
and we each night light Saint Elmo fires of the mind.
There are holes in the landscape, things gone
from the world's ongoing to which I cling
with my thousand atom fingers and I enter you
dazed by speed, touched by weightlessness.

I made holes in the landscape,
I got ahead of myself on the plain
between the mountains' glory and the milling
of orchards tendering their apples to paradise.
You are there, I know, hidden in the maples,
a radiant shawl wrapped round your zest for life,
there are stones in motion about us,
sanguine overhangs or shelters from the rain.
Yesterday we saw a desiccated lake and vines kneading
their bitter gritted memories,
and I took you again amidst midday laughter, your thighs
like soft cloth flashing a victory sign,
and I weightless before your splendour, falling
like a feather into the chasm of space-time.

Like a wearing away, holes in the landscape,
fissures in a mind razing the ground,
while you lift your voice to recall
that it's one's voice that best grasps the world,
summer's earth stirred up by a beast,
the grass gnawed and combed as
the plum tree lends winter its fruits.
You walk on through love's tremor
with the woman who opens her mouth and her blouse,
while thanks to her space dilates and assents
to gradients where joy probes light
and unearths it as did painters
of another day like Ozias Leduc
in Saint Hilaire, when the Catholic soul
laid its colours down on the land adored.

I made holes in the landscape, crumpled
the fabric of time-bound words,
tore up expanses of grass and cloth,
set foot in a fitfulness stoking
the body's passions and the mind's ordeals.
The October leaves smoulder low
in the solar seam of a main street
that a manic cat crosses scores of times down the afternoon,
but at night there are loosened ties, meanderings,
rose-flower scented pyjamas,
and your skin within that unfurls infinities
and lays claim to the balm of being loved.
I bring my mouth down to where your blood flows deep,
I taste of your suffering and serenities
and the plot line of happiness is summed up utterly
by my hand set down on your blazing breast.

And at times behind the scenes
there is a furrowed, mangled landscape
with a ragtag life in arrears,
sounds made in a café by a broken soul
where a father sits anguished in silence.
Yet families go laughing down the roads,
take snapshots of happiness in front of a lake
ringed round with clay and gravel
and all that sand in the undergrowth
where sleep fairies of last resort. But I find you
lying down in the ferns, your belly on damp leafage,
its heavenly sweetness that mounts in you
when the sky bears down on October's inferno,
to revive no more,
and the world in tatters sweeps up its shadows
and draws out into the night, ardent as ourselves.

It's always the same, empty or full,
absence and presence, we're forever returning
from eons of cares that have soaked the soul,
we emerge stunned onto shores
of bruised skin, beaches
of bristling hair that nobody combs,
we have raised ourselves up among the landscape's holes,
the small hollows, the voids that put us to the test.
I hold you, it's the height of heartbreak,
words course down loins, pummel the back of the neck,
there are great locutions etched on your back
for a novel not yet written
that will speak of our hopes for happiness under the trees
and in the mountain that empowers our shadows to speak
with the trees' flesh stirring our own,
our limbs' timber suddenly brought to life
poised between desire and doubt, oblivious
to the worst case statecraft that flouts the sun
and the particle ratios that will cause us pain.

Holes between each image, tunnels
through matter that binds us together and warms us,
heaps of waste from kitchens,
fields overturned to expose their sludge,
animals back from the city with scraps
of meat in their jaws, while I take
a road straight on, the wind diagonal,
swallowing dust and mortar
rising in a plume from work sites.
I see sand animals to the south,
deer to the north in a blizzard,
machines that comb through products
and frame their brainwashing every morning.
Where else to go with you who walk
garbed in autumn past the dry corn,
its metallic tremors lending
a soul to the countryside while far off
trucks at full volume growl,
and later in the night I love you despite
the commotion of animals and men,
and as if frightened of losing my substance
I fold myself one more time into your naked body.

And if the world does soldier on it's by the bye, in spite of all,
on the margins in noxious glosses,
exegeses without end of neuroses and sundry traumas,
ferried ever towards an overflow of woes,
those blights that make and unmake the night's
occurrence when a banal tsunami docks in Asia
and comes hither to tease our cold swathed feet,
in this age all fire all ice is assailed
by malefic intents and mutinies
while our nurturings cling to the here and now
before the wasted eyes of a child bidding us farewell.

And I chanced on the intoxication of distance,
felt my heart outside myself, content
to be exiled from my workaday thoughts,
scouring the countryside in search of sustenance.
It's in a gap between two apple trees
that the low sun gnawed at the sky's fleece
and the geese finished slicing into the blue.
It's there, beyond the woes continuing to grow
and the strident white-hot freeway
that I heard you singing,
and it was like a fault in the landscape,
the human voice a nest, a crucible
where I wanted to throw myself the better to hear you,
and yet I held back beneath a tree,
transfixed in that space caressed by your voice.

Openings, outlets, seepages,
the path leading to the woods, the repopulating
forest, affinities and sighs
at the core of families converted to happiness,
and your body tasting of humus and rare leafage,
there disclosing its cavities, its capricious distances
as if your hand beat out a clandestine tempo,
a cello unfurling endlessly its intervals,
exalted in its fifths, or this tearing
of the mystic flesh when desire
is a sudden erosion of our footings
that imparts an alien countenance to what is known.

In thought's woodland regions,
in the feral designs and the dereliction
of grace offered and withdrawn, of a happiness
striking so hard that it leaves me mute
and unmanned, undone in my inner being
as if to exist were no more than a series
of descents, of magical wanings, the afternoon
when the union of organs resolves itself in light
near to roseate at the approach of night
and your body exposed still holds me close
unable to explain its silence,
its elusive resolve like
a shawl wound round without start or end.

Holes in live matter, lakes whose water
would take flight along with clouds of barnacles,
missteps on earth-strewn pebbles
amid the porous quietude of a conversation
that resolves nothing of man's fate
nor of the times. The deafening embraces
have set aside peace and continuance,
and to survive the mudded moments is nothing,
the earth is imbued with an orange light
along a road where here and there
drift scraps of words, those of a father
to his daughter on a Sunday: "you should
concentrate more," as she hops, smiling,
from one stone to another, and I hold you to me
for a moment in this tepid light rising from the ground,
which in the boreal world blesses Novembers
bedded down in their sinking sun,
your body and mine unbolting space.

I made holes in the landscape like
lapses of memory or devotion.
I was distracted by your face and your voice,
and what I had once taken full to the body
suddenly melted away like a substance once thought supreme
in resistance and repudiation, those leaden weights,
my antithesis, dense lands
where stems can't reach their light.
I met air pockets on a flight path
towards what you described for no reason,
unbidden, employing art's lovely silences
and the intimate dimming of your smiling eyes.
I followed those signs, those thoughts, I lost
what I had ceased to be, having consigned time
to ruptured vessels from which it streamed.

I made tracks in my egress from anguish,
on a road that bears in on the bones
and plants foul tumors in the breast.
You were seated under one last tree
with the summer heat nipping away at its embers' dregs
and puffs of ash adrift
over ripe fruits and grilled meats.
You were reading poems to tame the wind,
and standing your ground with the hemiplegic choir,
your goodness bringing sick men to tears,
and through the illicit window I slipped into you
by way of heartrending songs,
splintering sadness into shards on the tiling
like a large sad glass of wine, the red
end point of suffering, a rampant red,
and I threw my old threadbare shirts to your feet
and my bloodless sentences that endlessly rewrote
the long saga of a past and its rare intoxications
that saw as hollow my prolixity in this century.

There was fencing, spaces between dogs
that allowed the dogs to call out to each other,
to gauge the strength of the other's anger
before responding. But among the trees
strewn through cold air peopled by dead flies
things transpired differently, in a collective
tremor of the highest limbs clinging
to the sky's fleece like an arboreal Parkinson's,
with a shaky hold on emptied nests
and with bygone feathers rippling through space,
and when cries of love resounded
you no longer knew what human thing still spoke out,
stark naked as man and woman in the shadows,
straying through a trade-off between body and being,
far flung sex honing in on its abode,
and the euphoria of a season that knew nothing
of humdrum sadness and the purée
or clay held to be form and truth.

And if you make holes in me, so much the better
and it's stronger than the mortar that holds me together,
bound to my shadows, welded to my ghosts.
If you grind me up or make of me an archipelago
that no longer knows its islands, like a land
whose far-flung regions, rugged, barely peopled,
ask themselves why they exist, I comb
through my residues of words, torn papers,
hard tables that bruise my elbows.
Is it me who finds you naked in the low light
of lavender scented sheets?
Is it me who reassembles himself each morning
and once more reconstructs the puzzle of his soul
with thoughts that return transfigured
and inner voyages seeking landfall
in your body's tempestuous port?

Glitches, hiccups in time's continuum,
as if it were conforming to the body's frailty
and the blackouts that at times bedevil
this landscape made by men, their plans
for grand devastation in the land of somnolent frogs,
while with you I must slowly retrace
the fractures' paths, wake up a hundred times
with in my gut the lost memory of languages learned
and submerge myself there once more seeking night music
with the tips of my fingers, the sweetness of restitched skin,
and the holes in the morning are sobs of joy
that I may harvest your tears
in this autumn's last scattering of earth at the base of its vines
and the fond warping of its anorexic apple trees,
and these are jolts, spasms on the fringes
of that saga delivering us to ourselves,
despite the configuration of errors and evil spells
and this sorrow leaving in limbo the tallying of our desires.

Holes in the landscape, scars in the flesh
of what's visible, all that in an embrace gives utterance,
exhalations come from afar, the disquiet of existing still,
sign language flaunted in the void between self and self,
fingers raised, thoughts, solar conjunctions,
so they go, migrating synapses burrowing down,
dislodging opaque hallways of thought.
You transport me through unknowing
and each night I rise seeking myself,
open books rife with murmur and fury,
you're stretched out in poems vast as life,
in the burning of Saint Theresa and *Rose éternité*.
It's November, no solstice or revolt, a stirring
of the little man tallying deaths and births,
with holes, the gnawing of fruits and leaves,
packed roads seeking a rest home,
and me stripped bare by cold and heat
that hail my body in their callous tongue,
your face rousing me from myriad winters.

And all at once this peopled desert, grassy
expanse, lawns sweeping away between here and there,
between your body on fire and the frigid river,
our long night's bed and the village squares
boasting dates and flags, always
at the close of a dark time's epic narratives.
We demand this resonance in our flesh, ever
afar, ever remote from its titanic decline,
mapped roads exceeding our intentions,
catalogues of heroic names, vivid stipplings
of memory and wide swathes
of silence between boundary stones, acres
of gone truth, reclaimed, the flaws
in the study of great philosophies, our steps
too discreet down the no man's land of an entire age.

The body's openwork fabric, a sieve of flesh
and blood on a November winter morning
as the light falls leaden onto gloom.
What is this void where once was passion,
these clods of clay that surface in the garden
under the paws of animals come out of the woods
perhaps frightened by the threadbare weft
of a season that has too soon shut its curtains?
What is it issuing forth from love,
this twilight panic, your dress forgotten
on the floor, bars of rain at the window?
But I hold you to me, we will lie
in the snow to fathom the sky's deeps,
we will share this fear of our aeon's arms
and like ghosts talk low
so as not to rouse its urge to demolish all.

We must start with that: pages
torn from the book, omissions, ellipses,
stammerings that give onto silences,
the mouth sewn tight in the cave where history roars.
I love you. I love you like a cry held in,
choked back, engulfed, buried mid-midriff,
you hear the landslip of old schoolbooks'
tales, strange fictions, allegories
of a memory that declares itself an august personage.
But it's not that, those are attritions,
the asphalt road that forgets its beginnings,
the hand that can no longer write, misbehaviour
in the dreary suburb hemmed in by corn.
It's the damaged narrative, the author's own oblivion
when the time comes to document sound and fury
and consign the fable's madness to judges and censors.

Descents, levellings. The word let drop
between us raises itself up, a squall, contortions,
memories that set the bedroom's drawers to trembling,
sound from the lamp that sizzles as you disrobe.
I shoulder my tasks, I make holes in winter,
a white shroud descending in mid-November,
there are anacolutha in destiny's sentences
and if I find sand beneath the bed, no one
will comprehend that I kneel to pray.
You are there, outstretched and naked, and I sense
great swathes of warmth, your eyes shut,
my languorous fingers foraging your fur,
an élan that rejigs humdrum time
and roams, radiant, the years' roads,
love arriving with its losses,
oblivions, its books forgotten on the table
and its promenades that prolong our awareness
of the woodlands' majesty, threads of snow
to which we consent to yield
while men's woes seeking refuge
beat on the nocturnal door.

A face of dust and ash, a body of smoke
reshaped by fingers that speak,
is it resurrection, is it to reconstitute
what was lost, friable matter,
torrents of molecules seeking a destiny?
You come at times at night to hear me sleep,
you ask yourself from what distance I have arrived.
I never cease returning as if I were
Bach's music, ribbons wafting,
wound round in our heads' white room,
winter's pilgrims on a German pathway
when your lips settle on my absent,
muddled brow. I who foretold my death in 2034,
having seen all, settled all, lived all,
here again are my sighs, my anguish, my shudderings,
my last finales with their creaking wood,
my words, my garments, my landscapes,
lost animals, small rodents all week long
under the roof, and you wake me with the reminder
that you love me and I burn in you with all
my former life that never stops replaying
the saraband of my fogged body,
back from its hot ashes, recalled
to its great, famished, openwork love.

Squirrel tracks dotting the snow,
the tree's claws on the cambered roof,
shadows, signs that there is an elsewhere,
that bodies have projects, projections
like your shoulders and the scarf around your neck
on a photo taken in Rome, Piazza Navona,
this extension of your beauty fronting the marble horses
that neigh, prone, wounded,
that moment in my non-existent past when you smiled,
the unseen man who snared your likeness,
absences, holes in the years' veneer
and myself arisen from nowhere, reappearing
among communities of books to embrace you.

Lacunae, my weaknesses, my deficits,
my calcified body chockablock with voids,
my presence fraught with orifices, cavities,
vaultings of well-being,
acrobatics of organs great and ravenous,
stroboscopes of desire and countless caresses,
intermittences, back and forths of laughter
and of sobbings that fissure my skull,
landscape, geography of all that's seismic,
you are my fast fracture, I rid myself
of me in you, of me in me.

These are not love poems,
merely storms in the tissue of time,
palpitations, rovings, clouds
of mosquitoes in a muddy forest
where we were on a June day, drops of rain
that console the thirsty, pebbles
with a sudden tenderness one for the other,
rock faults, crevices, bodily cavities
on mornings where life holds the road
and we set off once more on the path with a prayer within,
new phrases that reformulate the impossible,
skipped pages in the agenda of the living,
quantic appetites, songs suspended
over an unsuspected landscape
where animals dig holes in order to survive.

NOTES

Page 30. This poem cites two titles of philosophical works that I have often returned to in recent years: *Sources of the Self: The Making of the Modern Identity*, by Charles Taylor, Harvard University Press, 1989 (French translation, *Les sources du moi*, by Charlotte Melançon, Boréal, 1998), and *La mesure de l'homme*, by Daniel D. Jacques, Boréal, 2012.

Page 43. The first line, "Human life remains homeless," is a quotation from a book by the Czech philosopher Jan Patočka, *Heretical Essays in the Philosophy of History*, Carus Publishing, 1999.

Page 63. The title of the section "Dust and Ash" is inspired by the refrain of one of the poet Albert Lozeau's best known poems: "La poussière du jour et la cendre du jour..."

Signal
EDITIONS

CARMINE STARNINO, EDITOR
MICHAEL HARRIS, FOUNDING EDITOR

Robert Allen • James Arthur • John Asfour, trans.
Doug Beardsley • Paul Bélanger • Linda Besner
Walid Bitar • Marie-Claire Blais • Yves Boisvert
Jenny Boychuk • Asa Boxer • Susan Briscoe
René Brisebois, trans. • Mark Callanan • Chad Campbell
Edward Carson • Arthur Clark • Don Coles
Vincent Colistro • Jan Conn • Geoffrey Cook
Lissa Cowan, trans. • Judith Cowan, trans. • Mary Dalton
Ann Diamond • George Ellenbogen • Louise Fabiani
Joe Fiorito • Bill Furey • Michel Garneau • Susan Glickman
Gérald Godin • Lorna Goodison • Richard Greene
Jason Guriel • Michael Harris • Carla Hartsfield
Elisabeth Harvor • Charlotte Hussey • Dean Irvine, ed.
Jim Johnstone • D. G. Jones • Francis R. Jones, trans.
Virginia Konchan • Anita Lahey • Kateri Lanthier
R. P. LaRose • Ross Leckie • Erik Lindner • Michael Lista
Laura Lush • Errol MacDonald • Brent MacLaine
Muhammad al-Maghut • Nyla Matuk • Robert McGee
Sadiqa de Meijer • Robert Melançon • Robert Moore
Pierre Morency • Pierre Nepveu • Eric Ormsby
Elise Partridge • Christopher Patton • James Pollock
Michael Prior • Medrie Purdham • John Reibetanz
Peter Richardson • Robin Richardson • Laura Ritland
Talya Rubin • Richard Sanger • Stephen Scobie

Talya Rubin • Richard Sanger • Stephen Scobie
Peter Dale Scott • Deena Kara Shaffer
Carmine Starnino • Andrew Steinmetz • David Solway
Ricardo Sternberg • Shannon Stewart
Philip Stratford, trans. • Matthew Sweeney
Harry Thurston • Rhea Tregebov • Peter Van Toorn
Patrick Warner • Derek Webster • Anne Wilkinson
Donald Winkler, trans. • Shoshanna Wingate
Christopher Wiseman • Catriona Wright
Terence Young